OPOSSUMS!

A MY INCREDIBLE WORLD PICTURE BOOK

MY INCREDIBLE WORLD

Opossums are **marsupials**, which means they carry their babies in a pouch, just like kangaroos.

1

Opossums are primarily found in North and South America.

Although the names sound similar, American **opossums** are different than Australian **possums**.

There are over 100 different species of opossums, each with unique characteristics.

The Virginia opossum is the only marsupial native to North America.

Opossums are **nocturnal**, which means they are most active during the night.

They are **solitary** (prefer to be alone) and are not very territorial.

When threatened, opossums might play dead, a behavior called "playing possum."

They might even emit a foul-smelling odor to further convince predators.

Opossums are great climbers and can navigate through trees with ease.

They can live in a diverse range of habitats, from forests to grasslands to cities.

Opossums are **omnivorous**, which means they eat both plants and animals.

Their diet consists of insects, fruits, and small mammals.

Opossums have a keen sense of smell, which aids them in finding food.

They have distinctive pointed ears
that help them hear well.

Opossums have sharp teeth that enable them to eat a variety of foods.

They are good swimmers and
can cross rivers and streams
with ease.

Baby opossums are called **joeys** and are born very small and undeveloped.

They continue growing in their mother's pouch, and once big enough, they ride on her back!

Opossums communicate using vocalizations such as clicks, grunts, and hisses.

They are considered "living fossils" because they have changed very little in millions of years!

Opossums are incredible!

Made in the USA
Las Vegas, NV
11 December 2024

13880068R00017